HOPELESSNESS OF ARJUNA

(BASED ON BHAGAVAD GITA'S FIRST CHAPTER)

DR. JAGADEESH PILLAI

Contents

HOPELESSNESS OF ARJUNA

Bhagavad Gita Slokhas In English

Dedication

Dedicated to all those life situations, which I had to face in the battlefield of life, like; rejects, slaps, condemnation, which I overcame and the experiences helped me to understand the higher intelligence and wisdom of Supreme Spirit and this book as the outcome.

The Bhagavad Gita itself starts from an extreme despondency situation of a warrior Arjuna. Despite having all powers and efficiencies, his desires, attachments, etc., disturbs his mental stability, forgets his duties and actions and finally, he surrenders himself to Supreme to guide.

And the guide of wisdom and intelligence we have is "Bhagavad Gita"

About The Author

Dr. Jagadeesh Pillai *a voracious reader, Four Times Guinness World Record Holder, writer, and true research scholar was born in Varanasi, the abode of Lord Shiva. He is Ph.D. in Vedic Science. He is a multi-faceted polymath with innate qualities, creative ideas and many remarkable achievements. Although his roots extend back to "Gods own Country"(Kerala), the residents of Varanasi feel proud of him and adore him as a child of Varanasi who caters to every individual in need without any expectations. A deep study into his profile reflects that he has added so many feathers to his cap which makes him quite unique. He is a four times Guinness Book of World Records Holder in the following subjects :*

1.

   "Script to Screen" which he achieved by producing and directing a state of art animation film within the shortest time possible by breaking the earlier set record by Canadians. There are many national and international Awards and Recognitions to his credit.

2.

   Longest Line of Post Cards which he has done

on the occasion of 163 years of Indian Postal Day by 16300 post cards. The event was also connected with a questionnaire about Indian Flag.

3.

Largest Poster Awareness Campaign – This was achieved by designing an awareness campaign on the subject "Beti Bachao – Beti Padhao".

4.

Largest Envelop – Towards tribute to Prime Minister's initiative 'Make in India' – he has created about 4000 sq meter envelop using waste papers.

5.

Attempted by lighting 70000 candles on a 210 kg cake to celebrate the 70th Indian Independence day recorded in World Records India.

6.

Attempted a documentary on Dhamek Stupa of Sarnath dubbing in 17 languages, result is waiting from Guinness World Records.

He is versatile in Gita teaching. The young generation is fond of his Gita teaching and he has changed the life of many young through his continued motivational boost up and teachings.

.

He has composed and sung Gayatri Mantra in 1000 different tunes.

.

He has composed and sung Hanuman Chalisa in 108 different tunes.

.

He has composed and sung hundreds of Sanskrit Bhajans, Patriotic songs, etc.

.

He has written and directed so many short films and documentaries for awareness campaigns.

.

He has done voluntary services to UP Police and Kerala Police to spread awareness campaigns on the various issue through videos and photography.

He is on the path of authoring thousands of books on Indian culture, Indian Temples, and the life of extraordinary people.

It is hard to believe that he has produced and directed more than 100 Documentaries on a particular city (Varanasi) which is done by a single person.

He has helped and guided more than 25 boys and girls to achieve world records through various creative and innovative methods.

A multifaceted person who can apply the best of his intellect using the God-given blessings which have been showered upon every human being granting them an immense capacity to learn, experience, and experiment with many things and do wonders in this world of discrimination and disparities.

He is a teacher and a student at the same time

who always learns every day and teaches every day. As a master, his weakness was that he never sticks to a particular subject. Perhaps this weakness gives him the strength to master any area which he came across.

Each of his days dawned with learning a new topic and he spend most of his time experimenting and researching it.

He is also a selfless social activist and a motivational speaker.

His life was full of struggle, ups and downs, and failures. But he never gave up and faced all his trials and tribulations full of confidence. Today he is a successful young man with a lot of enthusiasm and rich life experience.

He has sung full Ram Charita Manas 51 hours audio by his own composition. He has also sung the whole Bhagavad-Gita in his own composition with a rhythmic background.

He has also sung "Lokah Samastha Sukhino Bhavantu" in 50 different languages.

Currently working on a detailed and scientific study on Veda, Upanishad, Puranas, Bhagavad Gita, etc.

Currently, he is the Hon' Chancellor of 'Eurasia Digital University'.

Awards

Four Times Guinness World Records
Winner of Mahatma Gandhi Vishwa Shanti Puraskar
Mahatma Gandhi Global Peace Ambassador
Kashi Ratna Award
Dr. APJ Abdul Kalam Motivational Person of the Year 2017
Mother Teresa Award
Indira Gandhi Priyadarshini Award
Bharat Vikas Ratna Award
Udyog Ratna Award
Vigyan Prasar Award
Poorvanchal Ratn Samman

PREFACE

Let me explain what inspired me to understand Gita and what motivated me to write this book through a crafted story. People have different experiences in life but here I am crafting a story of "stealing and thief".

If you are a person with a clear mind and clear intentions to do good for the society inspiring many great scholars and personalities or because of a voracious reader of many great inspiriting books.

You have already shown up your multiple talents and excelled in many fields. You are the inspiration for many youngsters.

After fulfilling all family obligations, you are entering into social service.

Suppose you are against the crime like "stealing" and don't like "thieves". You are trying to teach the thieves to stop the crime of stealing. You, being a responsible person, committed to doing good for the society, you are constantly selflessly involved to eradicate the crime of stealing and thieves. Social and administrative support is there and thousands of people around you, are very happy and satisfactory. Many thieves have changed their attitude of steeling and they have improved their lives because of you.

You are self-satisfied.

Full social support and their happiness are there.

There is no complaint against you in society rather wherever you go people will praise you for your attitude.

Thousands around you are eager to join you to get the teachings and motivation from you.

But there will be one or two persons in your life, maybe very close to you won't accept you. Instead of praising, they will abuse you. You are against the crime of stealing and thieves and working for it. But they will title you as the biggest criminal. They will never count your hundreds of good qualities, rather they will dig and dig and show you your shortcomings whether it does exist or not. Initially, you will also sock, will try to react, oppose and fight. You will try to show that you are clean and safe, but they will strengthen their attitude of abusing you so that you can step back and broke down. They may be highly jealous of you, maybe jealous because of your name and fame, jealous - because of your social acceptance, jealous - because of your social involvement, jealous - because of your helping nature.

You were working to eradicate thieves to stop the crime of stealing from society.

But those very few close people with you will project you as you are the biggest "thief" and will continuously abuse you and torture you.

Initially, you will shock and reacts, but later, since you are inspired by the life of many great personalities, you will stop reacting.

Then somebody in your life comes and teaches you that being a selfless social activist is/ not easy. Most of the people are selfish and want to be within their family of few people and friends. Whatever they do, think and collect will be for their family only. Their mind and thoughts are limited. This is called their physical involvement with the body and other physical entities. Their thought, imaginations and understanding level are limited to that only.

But, to become social irrespective of caste, creed, relationships, one has to become spiritual. Being, spiritual doesn't mean that you are a devotee of God and you do a lot of worshipping of many Gods and a regular visitor of temples, etc.

Spiritual means you understand the Soul (Jeevatma) within other being which is a part and particle of the Supreme Spirit and connected to the Supreme Spirit (Paramatma). Understanding the Soul and Supreme spirit is not that easy because they are invisible. That's why people will worship a physical entity of God like statues, pictures, etc. easily, though the statue and pictures are the creation of humans. They easily spent time and money on that.

Per the great scholars, understanding the Soul and Supreme Spirit is not easy and it cannot be achieved in one birth. This is called gradual spiritual development from birth to birth. Even a spiritually developed person in this birth might have also gone through physical attachments, desires, selfishness, etc. and later liberated from it birth by birth.

Even in Gita (7/3) says, thousands and thousands are trying to enter into the spiritual path (understanding Soul and Supreme Spirit) and thousands go in-depth to understand it and those thousands and thousands, only one understand me (means connection and power of the Soul and Supreme Spirit).

The above understanding will awake you and motivate you to understand yourself (spiritual way) and the other-self who are abusing you (physical way.

When the abusing and torture strongly continues, there are many chances of your breakdown by mind comes up. Then the Gita (6/5), explains to you that since you are in a high degree of spiritual development, consider all these oppositions as an examination to check the "balancing of your mind. Try to balance your mind more and more. Try to strongly maintain whatever others throw on you. If your mind disturbs, it will be like that you have created your enemy within you and this enemy will react, you will lose your intelligence and anything bad can happen. But to win the examination, you should practice silence. They oppose, reacts and shout on you means, their mind is disturbed and became their enemy. Whatever you do, good or bad, they will oppose and doubt you. Since you are practicing mental balancing and silence by not reacting, your mind will be calm, quiet and experience peace in mind. The intelligence of those people will be highly developed who has practiced mental balancing and find peace in mind even the situations around you are not pleasant.

Let me recall an incident....

A few years ago, when my BP was high, I was taken to a very famous Doctor of Banaras Hindu University who attends thousands of patients in a day. There was something special in his attitude or in his way of treating the patients. I never met him earlier and it was a chance for me to meet him. Since my wife was working in the same hospital; I could easily reach his room but it was overcrowded around the Doctor. It was a small room, no AC, just a fan, few Junior Doctors was also there to assist him. Because of the overcrowding of the patients, the atmosphere there was loud by their noises. It won't be easy for a common man to spend half an hour over there until he is a patient and forced to be there for treatment because the atmosphere was so unpleasant, discomfort and disturbing. I was waiting for my number to enter inside and waited outside for more than 10 minutes.

During those 10 minutes, I was watching the Doctor inside, how the Doctor might be attending this huge crowd of thousands of patients in a day sitting in the same place for more than 8 hours or so. Surprisingly, I was shocked to see him, his attitude and the way he was attending the patients. I was there for my check-up but instead, I was learning a big lesson of life over there. First of all, his nice smile constantly and his down to earth friendly attitude with the patients. The patients are there to tell that they are unhealthy, but he tells everybody that you are perfect by health, not un-healthy as you are imagining and you will become perfect very soon, no worry about it.

Such a so disturbing atmosphere, he was sitting and behaving as he is sitting in a resort in Switzerland on holiday and alone. Not even a 1% reaction to overcrowding or noisy atmosphere was reflecting on his face or in his attitude. Perfect balancing of mind I saw in him.

That day I decided to be like him and never my BP has to rise in the future, If you are an expert in mental balancing, you can win your health and many things. We are fighting to win people and things, which creates a un-satisfactory and disturbed mind. Through Un-necessary doubts, questioning, intervening in other's duties and actions and adamant to change others in my way, we develop pain, disappointments, etc. in our mind when we fail to achieve it.

It was very beautifully explained in Gita 4/40 – such people who doubt everything will never find peace in mind. Their opposing, abusing, doubting, etc. for necessary and unnecessary things clear that, their mind is unsatisfactory, disturbed, no mental balancing is there. Instead of concentrating their action, attitude, and developments, they will be chasing you, watching your movements, your actions and will try to find out the shortcoming of you regularly.

Then, how the teachings of mental balancing will get. No doubt, Krishna (The Supreme Spirit) is the best teacher. His teachings are actually to follow certain duties to be performed being human since the Soul as his part or particle are there in the body. He teaches that you are unaware of the real power and nature of you, your connection with me and what you should exactly be done while you are alive. To maintain creations and generations on the earth, many species are created and you are got the supreme form as human. But, instead of understanding and maintaining relationships with the creator (Supreme Spirit), being his Soul in our body, we forgot him and we made bondage, attachments with physical entities on the earth. Relations, attachment, bondage, etc. up to some limit is okay, beyond that there is no stability in it. Our living on the earth is limited to less than 100 years and any time before that you will be taken back whatever concrete relation you have with anybody on earth and whatever wealth you have accumulated over here will remain here or go waste. Did you ever think of why God has taken back the only child of parents in 8 years? Just imagine the concrete attachment and bondage the parents had with the child. We humans will be weeping when we hear this incident. It will be a heart-shocking incident for the parents that they lost their child. The pain will remain for years. But why God did that. We can see many such incidents around the world and many in our surroundings. Such incidents clearly warn us that, the creator only has the power on us and the creator has no respect for your attachments or bondage on relations. You are a person with a body, you are alive because Soul is there. The soul is connected with the mind and senses. Mind and senses are dirt because of many un-necessary attachments, bondage, desires, etc. The soul is there in the body to clean the mind and senses. Until the mind is completely cleaned, the Soul will be sent to earth through different bodies and in different locations. It will be like that you are learning from Class LKG to PhD. or D. Litt. You are there to learn and develop, not to make a concrete relationship with friends and other beings. Yes, you will meet many people like you and they will become your friends. But you should understand that they won't be there with you for long. Either they change their school, change their state, change their country for further studies. Same, Soul will be taken back and send to other bodies of any location, any family for further development of your mind and senses. (About attachment and bondage with relations is explained in Gita verses 13/9).

Once your mind and senses are 100% clean, The Supreme Spirit will take the Soul back and join him, and the Soul need not take any more birth and no further development and experience are required. But before finally taking a Soul back to him, and The Supreme Spirit gives you a 100% clean mind Certificate, you will be given many difficult tasks by giving more birth at different places with many adverse situations around you. As you are in a higher class, the task and situations will be tougher. In real life, if you are pursuing graduate studies, in college examination, no easy questions of class ten will be asked. The questions will be of higher degree and tougher.

The Mind has three types of qualities given by the Supreme, the lowest, medium and the highest. This has explained in detail in Chapter 14. You have to develop from the lowest, then to medium and from medium to highest. Once you are qualified 100% in the highest quality test, you will be able to achieve the Supreme quality and join with the Supreme Spirit. When you are practicing the highest quality level, your mind will be more cleaned and far away from the worldly pleasures and attachment with physical things. You will be more and more connected with the Soul. Even if you see a new person, you will be behaving politely with love as you are respecting the Soul within him and not you will dig his attitude and qualify of mind and senses, because it is not your duty to see good and bad in others. The Soul of others may be younger (junior) than you. For example, If a person nearby you are in the age of his 60s and you may be in your 30s in the present life. Since the 60-year-old person is eldest than you, you will respect him because of his age. Currently, Body-wise he is 60 years and you are 30 years. But we don't know the age of Soul. How many births each Soul has taken. Though, one's level of Spiritual Development, Intelligence Level, attitude, mental balancing we can determine whose Soul is senior. The 30 years old person might have taken more births than the 60-year-old person.

Again let's come back to the story which we started at the beginning of torturing you as a "thief". So the Guru, explained that your Soul is going through the highest examination of Spiritual Development. Here you will be given *the highest tests to check your mind's balancing and stability. Whatever you do, good or bad, somebody will be there to condemn it. The pressure of condemnation will be so high and high. Even if a little bit of mind balancing power is weak, you will be destroyed. For example, if you are associated with a political party and the other party in your opposition is in power. Since you are a politician and not in power, you will be condemning whatever good or bad the other party is implementing. You are not condemning the other party because they are doing everything badly. But since you are not in power and being a politician, you are forced to oppose it. There is a saying in South that "if you dislike your daughter-in-law, whatever she does will be condemned".*

But how one can practice 100% mental balancing and win the torture and such heavy condemnation from others.

Very beautiful teaching has given by Krishan in Gita (16/18) to overcome the situation very easily.

The word and sound are called "Shabda Brahma" because the words, sound, speech, thought, imagination, etc. are coming from the Soul, not from the Body. If there is a perfect body without a Soul, we call it a "dead body". No BODY can perform any activity without a Soul in it.

Soul (Jeevatma) is an extension of the Supreme Spirit (Paramatma, i.e. Krishna in Gita), we can say its "Krishna".

When somebody condemns you, the sound and words from others are coming from the Soul of others (who has a lower developed mind), and if you are listening to it means your Soul is listening to it. If you react badly (you are also lower developed). If you understood that and your mind balancing is at a higher level, you will reject it and maintain silence bypassing those condemnation words to the Soul within you. It means, the other person is not condemning or abusing you, rather they are abusing and condemning your Soul i.e. Krishna. Condemning Krishna means the other person is abusing Krishna and generating bad karma. The other person will excuse that he is condemned because he does not agree with the actions and attitudes of others.

If you are practicing the higher level of Soul development, you should be very careful to speak, respond, act, and react with others because any kind of reaction from you will be your reaction to the Supreme. If there is a mistake in your speech, words, and action, it means you are making mistakes in your answer sheet in an exam and you will be failed and will need to take re-exam.

If somebody condemns you, just imagine, they condemn Krishna not you as a person, that's all.

To continue with your actions and duties if you believe with your highly developed intelligence level and experience that you are doing well for the society, good for you and good for others.

If you are social and doing so many things for the benefit of others, people are happy, society, system, administration all are happy and praising you, then you are in a safe route. Still, if you find that one or few people condemns you by jealous, just bypass it to Krishna.

But if the society and a large number of people are unhappy, people are abusing you (not by somebody's jealous or ego, but because of your wrong attitude, wrong habits, ruins people and properties of the society and hurting people by wrongdoing) then you will be no longer survive. It means your mind and senses are ugly and not developed. If there are many serious continuous complaints against you from various people of the society it means you are a threat to the society, and your actions itself will ruin you and put in a very lower developed state of the soul.

If you are in a highly developed state of mind balancing and there is purity and clear good intentions in your actions, go ahead with it. Your examination is not to win a person, rather win Krishna (The Supreme Spirit). Your Soul examination paper will be verified by the Supreme Spirit (Krishna – Paramatma) itself, not by any person on the earth because no person on the earth is qualified to verify good and bad in your action. All humans are students of Krishna like you, not teachers. Nobody around you is qualified to evaluate you, except Krishna. For a person, an action done by you may be wrong, but in Krishna's perspective, it may be correct. Humans have limitations, selfishness, own interest, etc. to accept or reject an action done by you. So, whatever, you feel good, continue; let Krishna decide whether it was correct or wrong. Immense luck, blessings, mental piece, development of higher intelligence and wisdom, etc., in a future life or next birth depends, if you scored high for your good actions. Hurdles, mental agony, hindrances, losses, etc. happens if you have scored less for your wrong actions. That's why on 2/47

Krishna says ...

"KARMANYEVADHIKARASTE MAA PHALESHU KADAACHANA

MAA KARMAPHALAHETURBHOORMAA TE SANGOSTWAKARMANI"

"you are only entitled to perform your action without expecting the fruit of it and should have an intention to experience the fruit of it". What fruit should be given, when, where and how all depend on Krishna. You just try your best to perform your duties.

Your level of mental balancing peace Your future life and next birth According to the result of Krishna's verification of your examination paper and per the marks obtained

When the mind feels higher pain, Krishna will give you the highest teaching to balance the mind and win your mind. There is the highest pain of Arjuna is described in the first chapter of Bhagavad Gita that's why the name of the first chapter is "Arjuna VishadaYoga" –

"Despondency of Arjuna" – Arjuna, a Soul with the body with a dis-balanced mind. The word "Vishada" itself is taken from the Verses 1/28).

ॐ

Understand Krishna & Arjuna

Who gets tired in war while fighting? – The warrior (Arjuna). His mind and body both are restless.

To regain strength, the warrior needs rest at night. When the warrior is going in his shelter for rest, the Guru (Krishna) enters there to motivate him and transfer wisdom and knowledge.

"Wisdom and knowledge by the Guru" cool his restless mind and "sleep with a relaxed mind" at night, cool the body and ready for the flight the next day with full strength.

Krishna means in Sanskrit – Dark, Night and Darkness

Arjuna means in Sanskrit – Day, Light and Whiteness

The Krishna of darkness enters at night and cool and relaxes the mind of Arjuna (whiteness).

Again...

Krishna – Dark - Supreme

Arjuna - light - Soul (with mind and senses)

When there is darkness or restlessness in the Soul because of the ignorant actions and desires of mind and senses (fight), to cool down the Soul with wisdom and intelligence, the Supreme enters.

No King alone can lead a kingdom. The power of King and the intelligence and wisdom of the Guru is required to establish goodness and well being.

Intelligence and wisdom remove ignorance.

In the last verses of Gita, Sanjay mentions the same as above, where there is an intelligent Guru and dedicated powerful disciple is there, where righteousness, real justice, peace, and harmony exists.

Dr. Jagadeesh Pillai
(Four Times Guinness World Record Holder,
Winner of Mahatma Gandhi Vishwa Shanti Puraskar,
Author of Many Books)

HOPELESSNESS OF ARJUNA

Yes, we know that every book has chapters, but here, the most important part of Gita is the title name of this Chapter. There are two most important words in the first chapter's title:-

1. ARJUNA (Name of a Person – represents us)

2. VISHADA (state of disappointment or depression-like we all face at the time of distress).

"ARJUNA" represents all of us, all the people on the globe earth. But here per the title of the Chapter, "ARJUNA" is a person who is very confused and is depressed or in despondency.

"VISHADA" or despondency is a state of a person, when he/she is suffering from depression, disappointments, confusion, doubts, etc. or even in the mid of an unmanageable situation.

So, now one thing is clear that this holy book of Bhagavad Gita starts from a situation where a person "ARJUNA" (represents all of us) has some confusion, doubts and in a depressed state ("VISHADA"), like most of us are facing in our life.

When we are unable to manage adverse situations in life, it leads to physical (health problems) and psychological disturbances in life. Even if it is physical or psychological, we normally consult a doctor for medications to recover from it. Sometimes it works, sometimes it doesn't. Many people are even committing suicides when they are having an adverse situation in life which goes beyond its extreme or uncontrollable by them.

That's the reason I called the book Bhagavad Gita as "MOTIVATIONAL GITA", as I understood that Bhagavad Gita is an ocean of motivational lectures (universal law) by the supreme spirit to overcome the obstacles that we face in our day-to-day life, to overcome all despondencies in our life and lead a harmonious life by balancing the imbalances happening throughout our life.

When we buy a product from the market, say, an electronic product, it accompanies with a user manual to understand its operation. Without a user manual, we will try to operate it in our way and because of manipulating the operations by ignorance; the product will start creating problems and won't work smoothly and will soon ask for a repair, and eventually, after some time it becomes damaged which will ultimately create disturbances.

Apart from that, to become a professional consultant like a Doctor, an Engineer, an Architect, etc. we need to learn it professionally from the respective masters to master in those fields. Without proper learning, we cannot perform well in that field.

So, there are two things I would like to emphasis here,

1. A user manual is required to understand the proper operation of a product.

2. We need professional qualifications and experience to perform in a respective field of activity that we choose as our career.

Bhagavad Gita also represents as a user manual for humans and its teachings are meant to perfectly perform our duties and activities throughout our life by facing and overcoming all kinds of imbalances that come during the long-term of our life. It's a user manual for us - for we humans to understand the secrets and truths of our self-existence and the duties must be performed in complimentary by the rule of nature because we humans are also a part of nature. So the creator of the universe or nature has its own rules which the creations including human beings must follow.

Now let's check the first sloka (verse) of the first chapter of "Bhagavad Gita".

DHARMA KSHETRE KURUKSHETRE

SAMAVETA YUYUTSAVAHA

MAMAKAAHA PANDAVA CHAIVA

KIM KOORVATA SANJAYA

Let me clarify before we proceed further:

DHARMA – The Goodness within us (Positivity, Obligatory Duties)

KURU - Evil thoughts and activities within us. (Negativities)

KSHETRA – Place of activity or action (Our own body) -

WHERE THE WAR HAPPENS - Between good and evil thoughts (family of thoughts).

The above verse is a question that is asked by Dhritarashtra (a blind person – with a blind and ignorant mind) to Sanjya, who through his clairvoyance powers explains the happenings on the battlefield of Kurukshetra.

Please concentrate on the meaning of the first line of the first verse "Dharma Kshetre - Kurukshetre"

Usually, we see that the war takes place between two dynasties, two countries, two states, etc. But here, the war happens within the same family, in the same battlefield.

His question doesn't mean that what happened between "Dharma" and "Kurus".

Whereas,

The actual meaning of his question is - What happens to the Kshetra of Dharma when Kurus enters.

The battlefield (Kshetra) is our body itself.

Let me explain it to you once again with a few examples:

DHARMA KSHETRA (Kshetra of Dharma – Place of Positivity)

Explanation:

(Positive thoughts, actions, attitude, sacrifices, forgiveness, balancing situations, performing obligatory duties for the well being of all other beings in the world, etc. are referred to as Dharma)

KURU KSHETRA (Kshetra of Kurus – Place of Negativities)

Explanation:

(Negative thoughts, actions, attitudes, desire, lust, anger, ego, jealousy, attachments, competitions for luxury and to accumulate limitless properties and comforts, etc. are referred to as Kurus)

The Place or the Kshetra is our own BODY.

(Detail explanation available about Kshetra (body) in Chapter- 13)

Explanation:

The conflict begins in a family when Negativities enters in the place of Positivity. The power and influence of negativities will diminish the goodness and positivity, because of ignorance of some rules of nature, we easily come under the influence of negativities. When negativities within us increase, it leads to a gradual decrease in positivity, and thus, problems, confusion, doubts, stress, disappointment, etc. arises in our life.

For example, just imagine the stage of our infancy, a newborn baby, or an 'infant' – is in a stage where the infant's body is full of positivity (goodness) within it. *(That's why up to some childhood age, we in India used to consider the child as God).* The baby is unknown about its existence, the name of the parents and even about any of the happenings around the world. The infant even doesn't know about the competitions or the race occurring in the world. It's mind, heart and soul are not even having a single drop of "Kurus" - negativity.

But, when the infant, gradually grows up in the stereotype and the prejudiced atmospheric environments of the surroundings, the infant's innocent body with full of positivity gradually afflicted with so many negativities because of the of "Maya" or "Illusions" (The infant eventually gets attracted and adapts the happening from the surroundings).

When the infant enters the real world and starts to understand the world, many of the negative entities like ego, desire, lust, hatred, jealousy, etc. (these negatives entities are referred to as "Kurus" in on word), starts to develop within him. When he is unable to satisfy his desire or expectation, it leads to depression, disappointment.

When the child enters his teenage, he has to decide about his career and to start planning for his future. At this stage, so many questions and confusions come up day by day, and mostly the confusions stand for a long time which again leads to depression and disappointment. The situation of the boy is the same as Arjuna in the first chapter. So, we can conclude that from the teenage onwards, the child is in the situation of "Confused Arjuna", because he enters into the reality of life, where he has to take en-number decisions for his future. But, the surroundings will confuse him in many ways that he wouldn't be able to reach a final destination of his plan of life.

Now, his Kshetra (Body) has divided into two sections within it:-

1. Dharma – (Good) - Positivity

2. Kurus – (Evil) - Negativities

And from here onwards throughout the life, the battle between "Good" and "Evil" within us will go on, and on so many occasions in our life, we will experience failures and dejections. At this stage, we will give up and step back, because of the ignorance of the "rule of nature" or we do not follow a user manual to successfully lead the life.

To manage such adverse situations and to win the struggles in anybody's life, the motivational teachings of Bhagavat Gita (the universal law) will help and encourage.

ॐ

So, to understand Bhagavat Gita, we have to imagine our own body as the battlefield and the soul within us as Krishna (Jeevatma - a part of the supreme spirit). When we compare the same with the universe, the creator of the universe itself is Krishna and thus the Krishna explains the universal law which has to be followed by every human being.

Only humans have given immense power, intelligence, and wisdom. All other living beings follow the universal law "as it is" because they haven't given such extra intelligence like humans and even if they have little, their power has been limited to some extent and they cannot think or act beyond that limit. They all are acting like a battery fitted electronic doll, it will act as per factory settings, not beyond that.

But a human can go beyond any level. But most of the humans forget that we are a part of the universe and we have to live per universal law, instead, they become masters of their own and trying to manage life and situations in their way without understanding the universal reality.

I wish to share an example to understand the above little more clearly. Let's imagine the Universe as a 10 TB Hard Disk. All universal secrets are there in the Hard Disk. Some secrets like Gravity etc. the scientists have discovered already and till millions of secrets are there in the universe. For example, still, we need to discover a way to easily purify the seawater and we still need to find out a solution to immediately destroy plastic, there may be many scientists working on it. But the universe knows the secret, we need to explore it through a continuous process of discovery.

What I want to explain is like 10 TB hard disk representing complete universe with all secrets within it, we have a 10 TB memory card, with the complete copy of materials what we have in the 10 TB Hard Disk. In short, there are one 10 TB Hard Disk & one 10 TB memory card and complete universal secrets are the contents in it. In spiritual language, we can say 10 TB Hard Disk as "STHOOLA PRAKRUTI" which can be seen and the 10 TB Memory card as "SOOKSHMA PRAKRUTI".

10 TB Hard Disk is the Universe Itself – The Para Brahma

10 TB Memory card is our soul within us - The Jeevatma

The Jeevatma (the soul within us) knows all the secrets of the Para Brahma (the universe), that's why scientists or the people who are in the process of discovery can discover many universal secrets. When one person or a scientist is there on his continuous process of discovery, one day his soul will reveal the secret to him like we search something on the computer putting a word on the search box.

In Bhagavat Gita, there is only one verse, the first verse in which Dhritarashtra asks Sanjaya who is the mediator communicator between Krishna and Dhritarashtra. After the first sloka nowhere, Dhritarashtra asks anything. He is in silent mode. Instead, Arjuna, asks questions by questions to Krishna and trying to improvise and purify him from his misunderstandings and ignorance.

Even in our today's life, in our surroundings also we can see many persons like Dhritarashtra who are blind, selfish and don't need anybody's advice. Because he is in power as king and thinking & worrying about his children, family, and kingdom.

Dhritarashtra was silently listening and watching, whether Krishna is revealing any special trick to Arjuna which may be used to kill my sons and conquer my kingdom. He was never worried about removing his ignorance and of his children. This shows his extreme attachment towards his family and power as King.

In some texts, the name "Dhritrashtra" is explained as "Sitting on a Chair of a Nation", "Dhrit" which means "Chair", "Rashtra" means "Nation". We can imagine the political fighting for "the chair". Nobody wants to leave the Chair of Power. To be there on the Chair, many political, ethical and unethical games are playing by the politicians.

As mentioned in the beginning, the infant which has only positivity within him gradually starts with many attachments and worldly pleasures as he grows up. He will have an attachment to many good things and bad things. He may like milk to drink and at the same time, he may like to drink alcohol too. He may have many friends with a positive attitude and he may have many friends with a negative attitude. However, for him, all are his friends and he has an attachment with both kinds of his friends.

In the first chapter sloka, 4 to 6 mentions the fighters on Pandava's side with their skills and sloka 7 to 9 mentions the fighters on Kaurava's side with their skills.

We can understand the above like....there is high-density negativities exists within us and at the same time we have high-density positivities are also existed.

Parents are forcing his son to stop taking Alcohol and advising to take Milk. But the son has an attachment with both. He wants to take milk while at home when he is with parents, but when he is in parties with friends, he wants to take Alcohol. Since the son has the attachment with both Milk and Alcohol, the parents force him to stop alcohol and that force on him gets into the state of despondency.

Whenever situations like despondency, depression, stress, confusion, doubt, etc. generate within us and life becomes so difficult and uncomfortable. Such situations lead to physical and psychological disturbances in life.

In life, we have to meet many persons and to face many situations and most of the people quickly get down by depression or disappointments. Most of them have no courage to face and fight with the situations and overcome them. When the situation gets worse and worse, some people even commit suicide.

An Important Quote to Note....

Whenever we discuss Bhagavad Gita and when we start following it or advise others to read and follow it, many people will object and warn us not to read it because it will force us to sacrifice the daily living, family living and will force one to become a Saint.

Arjuna (in the first chapter - verse 32) asking Krishna that he doesn't want to win the battle, he has no interest in the Kingdom and he is ready to sacrifice all life pleasures, etc. and for that, he is not ready to fight.

Here, Arjuna is ready to become a Saint because he is ready to sacrifice everything but not ready to fight to achieve it. If the reason of Bhagavad Gita was to force one to become a Saint, the next chapters of Krishna's teachings would not have happened and Krishna might bless him here to become a Saint. Rather, Krishna motivates him to fight back to kill the evils and retain the goodness and achieve everything.

In the last chapter (Chapter 18, Verse 73), we can see, what ultimately Arjuna gained, whether he becomes a Saint or he becomes an energetic, enthusiastic, highly intelligent warier who understand the deep teachings of Krishna and promises and agrees to fight back all evils to retain goodness within and around him.

So finally, in the first chapter, ARJUNA represents all of us or the disappointed or distressed people who are unable to overcome the negative situations in life and mentally get down and get back from life as ARJUNA sits down and asked Krishna that he is unable to fight.

So if anybody thinks that life is full of struggles and has to face many adverse situations, this Motivational Gita will pave the way to overcome it, excel and succeed in every field of life.

Again a little more explanation to understand the name "ARJUNA". Even in this first Chapter, Arjuna is disappointed and in depression, but his name not match with his that attitude. Arjuna means "who can win", "who can gain", "who can lead", "who can generate", "who can think", "who can fight", "who can overcome" – that's why I mentioned earlier that "ARJUNA" represents we all human being who can "win" and "overcome" everything.

So now let's imagine that we are a group of depressed, confused, disappointed persons are gathered and waiting in an auditorium for the motivational speaker to come. Here the motivational speaker is Krishna (the universal lawmaker, and we, his creations, are forced to follow his law), he through his speech, will explain about the law, how to follow, how to face bad situations and such so many things to remove our ignorance and to re-charge us to fight back and win in our life.

Bhagavad Gita Slokhas in English

For Quick Reference

1

dhritarashtra uvacha
dharma-kshetre kuru-kshetre samaveta yuyutsavah
mamakah pandavashchaiva kimakurvata sanjaya

2

sañjaya uvācha
dṛiṣhṭvā tu pāṇḍavānīkaṁ vyūḍhaṁ duryodhanastadā
āchāryamupasaṅgamya rājā vachanamabravīt

3

paśhyaitāṁ pāṇḍu-putrāṇām āchārya mahatīṁ chamūm
vyūḍhāṁ drupada-putreṇa tava śhiṣhyeṇa dhīmatā

4, 5, 6

atra śhūrā maheṣhvāsā bhīmārjuna-samā yudhi
yuyudhāno virāṭaśhcha drupadaśhcha mahā-rathaḥ
dhṛiṣhṭaketuśhchekitānaḥ kāśhirājaśhcha vīryavān
purujit kuntibhojaśhcha śhaibyaśhcha nara-puṅgavaḥ
yudhāmanyuśhcha vikrānta uttamaujāśhcha vīryavān
saubhadro draupadeyāśhcha sarva eva mahā-rathāḥ

7

asmākaṁ tu viśhiṣhṭā ye tānnibodha dwijottama
nāyakā mama sainyasya sanjñārthaṁ tānbravīmi te

8

bhavānbhīṣhmaśhcha karṇaśhcha kṛipaśhcha
samitiñjayaḥ
aśhvatthāmā vikarṇaśhcha saumadattis tathaiva cha

9

anye cha bahavaḥ śhūrā madarthe tyaktajīvitāḥ
nānā-śhastra-praharaṇāḥ sarve yuddha-viśhāradāḥ

10

aparyāptaṁ tadasmākaṁ balaṁ bhīṣhmābhirakṣhitam
paryāptaṁ tvidameteṣhāṁ balaṁ bhīmābhirakṣhitam

11

ayaneṣhu cha sarveṣhu yathā-bhāgamavasthitāḥ
bhīṣhmamevābhirakṣhantu bhavantaḥ sarva eva hi

12

tasya sañjanayan harṣhaṁ kuru-vṛiddhaḥ pitāmahaḥ
siṁha-nādaṁ vinadyochchaiḥ śhaṅkhaṁ dadhmau
pratāpavān

13

tataḥ śhaṅkhāśhcha bheryaśhcha paṇavānaka-gomukhāḥ
sahasaivābhyahanyanta sa śhabdastumulo 'bhavat

14
tataḥ śhvetairhayairyukte mahati syandane sthitau
mādhavaḥ pāṇḍavaśhchaiva divyau śhaṅkhau
pradadhmatuḥ

15
pāñchajanyaṁ hṛiṣhīkeśho devadattaṁ dhanañjayaḥ
pauṇḍraṁ dadhmau mahā-śhaṅkhaṁ bhīma-karmā
vṛikodaraḥ

16, 17, 18
anantavijayaṁ rājā kuntī-putro yudhiṣhṭhiraḥ
nakulaḥ sahadevaśhcha sughoṣha-maṇipuṣhpakau
kāśhyaśhcha parameṣhvāsaḥ śhikhaṇḍī cha mahā-rathaḥ
dhṛiṣhṭadyumno virāṭaśhcha sātyakiśh chāparājitaḥ
drupado draupadeyāśhcha sarvaśhaḥ pṛithivī-pate
saubhadraśhcha mahā-bāhuḥ śhaṅkhāndadhmuḥ pṛithak
pṛithak

19
sa ghoṣho dhārtarāṣhṭrāṇāṁ hṛidayāni vyadārayat
nabhaśhcha pṛithivīṁ chaiva tumulo abhyanunādayan

20
atha vyavasthitān dṛiṣhṭvā dhārtarāṣhṭrān kapi-dhwajaḥ
pravṛitte śhastra-sampāte dhanurudyamya pāṇḍavaḥ
hṛiṣhīkeśhaṁ tadā vākyam idam āha mahī-pate

21, 22
arjuna uvācha
senayor ubhayor madhye rathaṁ sthāpaya me 'chyuta

yāvadetān nirīkṣhe 'haṁ yoddhu-kāmān avasthitān
kairmayā saha yoddhavyam asmin raṇa-samudyame

23
yotsyamānān avekṣhe 'haṁ ya ete 'tra samāgatāḥ
dhārtarāṣhṭrasya durbuddher yuddhe priya-chikīrṣhavaḥ

24
sañjaya uvācha
evam ukto hṛiṣhīkeśho guḍākeśhena bhārata
senayor ubhayor madhye sthāpayitvā rathottamam

25
bhīṣhma-droṇa-pramukhataḥ sarveṣhāṁ cha mahī-
kṣhitām
uvācha pārtha paśhyaitān samavetān kurūn iti

26
tatrāpaśhyat sthitān pārthaḥ pitṝīn atha pitāmahān
āchāryān mātulān bhrātṝīn putrān pautrān sakhīṁs
tathā
śhvaśhurān suhṛidaśh chaiva senayor ubhayor api

27
tān samīkṣhya sa kaunteyaḥ sarvān bandhūn avasthitān
kṛipayā parayāviṣhṭo viṣhīdann idam abravīt

28
arjuna uvācha
dṛiṣhṭvemaṁ sva-janaṁ kṛiṣhṇa yuyutsuṁ samupasthitam
sīdanti mama gātrāṇi mukhaṁ cha pariśhuṣhyati

29, 30, 31

vepathuśh cha śharīre me roma-harṣhaśh cha jāyate
gāṇḍīvaṁ sraṁsate hastāt tvak chaiva paridahyate
na cha śhaknomy avasthātuṁ bhramatīva cha me manaḥ
nimittāni cha paśhyāmi viparītāni keśhava
na cha śhreyo 'nupaśhyāmi hatvā sva-janam āhave

32, 33

na kāṅkṣhe vijayaṁ kṛiṣhṇa na cha rājyaṁ sukhāni cha
kiṁ no rājyena govinda kiṁ bhogair jīvitena vā
yeṣhām arthe kāṅkṣhitaṁ no rājyaṁ bhogāḥ sukhāni cha
ta ime 'vasthitā yuddhe prāṇāṁs tyaktvā dhanāni cha

34, 35

āchāryāḥ pitaraḥ putrās tathaiva cha pitāmahāḥ
mātulāḥ śhvaśhurāḥ pautrāḥ śhyālāḥ sambandhinas tathā

etān na hantum ichchhāmi ghnato 'pi madhusūdana
api trailokya-rājyasya hetoḥ kiṁ nu mahī-kṛite

36, 37

nihatya dhārtarāṣhṭrān naḥ kā prītiḥ syāj janārdana
pāpam evāśhrayed asmān hatvaitān ātatāyinaḥ
tasmān nārhā vayaṁ hantuṁ dhārtarāṣhṭrān sa-
bāndhavān
sva-janaṁ hi kathaṁ hatvā sukhinaḥ syāma mādhava

38, 39

yady apy ete na paśhyanti lobhopahata-chetasaḥ
kula-kṣhaya-kṛitaṁ doṣhaṁ mitra-drohe cha pātakam

katham na jñeyam asmābhiḥ pāpād asmān nivartitum
kula-kshaya-kritam dosham prapashyadbhir janārdana

40
kula-kshaye praṇashyanti kula-dharmāḥ sanātanāḥ
dharme naṣhṭe kulam kritsnam adharmo 'bhibhavaty uta

41
adharmābhibhavāt krishṇa praduṣhyanti kula-striyaḥ
strīṣhu duṣhṭāsu vārṣhṇeya jāyate varṇa-saṅkaraḥ

42
saṅkaro narakāyaiva kula-ghnānām kulasya cha
patanti pitaro hy eṣhām lupta-piṇḍodaka-kriyāḥ

43
doṣhair etaiḥ kula-ghnānām varṇa-saṅkara-kārakaiḥ
utsādyante jāti-dharmāḥ kula-dharmāsh cha śhāśhvatāḥ

44
utsanna-kula-dharmāṇām manuṣhyāṇām janārdana
narake 'niyatam vāso bhavatītyanuśhuśhruma

45, 46
aho bata mahat pāpam kartum vyavasitā vayam
yad rājya-sukha-lobhena hantum sva-janam udyatāḥ
yadi mām apratīkāram aśhastram śhastra-pāṇayaḥ
dhārtarāṣhṭrā raṇe hanyus tan me kshemataram bhavet

47
sañjaya uvācha

evam uktvārjunaḥ saṅkhye rathopastha upāviśhat
visṛijya sa-śharaṁ chāpaṁ śhoka-saṁvigna-mānasaḥ

CONTACT

Phone & Whatsapp

9839093003

Email : myrichindia@gmail.com

facebook.com/dr.jagadeeshpillai

facebook.com/dr.jagadeeshpillaiofficial

Youtube.com/drjagadeeshpillai

ॐ